POEMS
AND
TRANSLATIONS

LADSON
BRIGHT

UNITED WRITERS PRESS
ASHEVILLE, N.C.
2026

Published by
United Writers Press
Asheville, N.C. 28803

ISBN: 978-1-961813-96-0 (trade paper)

All images, including cover art, are courtesy of the author. The photograph accompanying the poem "Mediterranean Scene," pg. 75, is of a painting by J. Burnett which belongs to the author.

Printed in the USA.

To My Wife

Acknowledgments

In preparation for this book of poems, I am thankful to my wife Joanmarie Bright for her inspiration and assistance. Special thanks go to Dr. John Hrebik, of my former college, Cape Fear Community College, for his invaluable and considerable attention to—and extensive comments on—these poems. I also thank Jerry Clark for his help with manuscript preparation.

Table of Contents

Religious Poems

Poems of Love and Loss

HAIKU and Other Poems

Translations

POEMS
AND
TRANSLATIONS

RELIGIOUS
POEMS

But now being made free from sin, and
become servants to God, ye have your
fruit unto holiness, and in the end,
everlasting life.
—Romans 6:22 (KJV)—

May these lines herein
give God praise and acclaim,
and be an aid to fruit in holiness
in His sacred name.

"If we but turn to God,
that itself is a gift of God."

—St. Augustine—

TURNING GODWARD

Turning Godward is the first need of the soul,
a gift that turns our darkness into light,
to open then ourselves to His control,
and from division focuses our sight.

A second gift and miracle gives Christ,
from Father's love within the Trinity,
who for our sins (O blessed sacrifice!) sufficed,
shares with believers His eternity.

As third and other gifts, the Holy Spirit imparts
varied abilities as He indwells,
for us to give to others from our hearts
a love that, like a current, so upwells.

Thus blessed with threefold gifts of our awakening,
let us sing out our praises unto God our King!

DEPTH OF LOVE

Lord, when we dig for treasure in the earth,
And get but fragments of your joys that last,
We find in us a most lamented dearth
As mirrored in these shards, we peer aghast.
Love's archaeologists, we seek rebirth,
In depths of hope held in your arms nailed fast,
And there discover all our beings' worth:
Eternal future from a buried past.
Indeed, Lord, *You* dig down deep for all,
Bringing such treasure from your heaven above,
Removing crusts that here keep minds in thrall,
Sowing in place of brokenness your love.
    The way of doubt is dark, and yet we see
    The arms that pick us up and pull us free.

A Woven Life

There was a path I could not find
in that small mill town in my mind.
When I was barely out of womb,
the sound of shuttle and of loom
began my family's day;
and then my father went away
to war—and then again at his return.
In looking back I sometimes yearn
to know what other paths might have begun,
to find what other fortunes might have spun
from that departure. What if life
splits all our unique moments like a knife,
so from each fragment emanates a whole
with different patterns to become our role?
Or are we guided by a larger scope,
Steadfastly waiting for the blessèd hope?
In recent ripeness I can better see
a different Father who's been there for me
through all the strivings of my life to be
the Lord and Weaver of my destiny.

"For now we see in a mirror dimly,
but then face to face. Now I know
in part, then I shall know fully, even
as I have been fully known."

—1 Cor 13:12—

Preparations

We are not made to see at once the love,
the truth and splendor of the Lord above.
Our view is clouded by the depth of sin;
the part and not the whole comes into ken.

Show mercy unto those who doubt, says Jude;
See in a mirror credence that is crude.
Surpass in growth and knowledge based in Him,
and persevere in love when all looks dim.

He is the light Who in our darkness shines,
Who shared our humanness and dross refines.
Soul's mirror will be cloudy then no more;
The husk be winnowed, showing then the core.

May we, prepared by undeservèd grace,
Behold with clarity His blessèd face.

KNOWLEDGE

God in His image made us and the tree
of knowing good and evil. Bitterly,
we ate of it in order to be wise,
and now we know of death as one who dies.

How we disgraced His image is a shame.
Wrong choice and disobedience were to blame.
Yet still some of His image we retain
to see more fully when He comes again.

His might and glory will we see Him show,
and, sin's dominion broken, His face know.

On the Love of Christ

Not golden streets, nor music of the spheres,
Nor infinite expanse of space above
Could reach into this world of flesh and fears
To draw us as does your enfolding love.

Lord Jesus, on the hard wood of your Cross
You gave your Blood and Body that we'd know
That we must hence fear nothing but your loss;
That now, clothed in your Spirit, we shall grow.

Help us reach forth that others may know you,
How over death you rose to make us free;
May we, though sinners, let your love shine through,
To share the joy of your eternity.

Love's irony—such sinners saved from sin
By arms nailed fast that yet could take us in.

On Holy Saturday

Tumult of Earth and Hell when thou did'st die,
Ceases, with agony of death now past;
There comes a promised hope, bright victory
Accomplished now within souls' reach at last.

But where art thou, truly, Lord, this Holy Saturday?
Thy Father's bosom always holds thee fast, it's true.
But thou a journey first dost make this day,
In depths of suffering giving Hell its due.

Perhaps some worthy souls detained in Hell,
Were harrowed heavenward by thy holy might;
Thy width and reach of mercy done so well
Could bring some lost ones out of deadly night.

With thy triumphant rise over sin's sway,
Thy risen glory lights our Easter Day.

ORDERED LIVES

Order our lives so, O Lord, that we
May know the quiet beauty of thy will.
Direct us in our ways that we may be
Attentive and harmonious and still.

We struggle often, lose our way at times;
We fail to listen to thy Voice within.
Thy guidance, Lord, protect us from those crimes
That we commit against thee when we sin.

Dispose our hearts, O Lord, to thy control;
Give us steadfast assurance of thy love;
With thy compassion, Father, make us whole
And lead us to thy joyous realm above.

Wherein, in ordered peace, we'll see thy face,
And know the fullness of thy precious grace.

When I read the several dates of the Tombs, of some that died Yesterday, and some six hundred Years ago, I consider that great Day when we shall all of us be Contemporaries; and make our Appearance together.

—Addison, *The Spectator*, No. 26—

Sin is inevitable, but all shall be well, and all shall be well, and all manner of thing shall be well.

—Julian of Norwich,
Revelations of Divine Love, ch. 27—

JUDGMENT DAY

What a day it shall be when dead men rise!
Though all be one as contemporary,
Not all, it is said, will attain to the skies;
A different fate will be judged necessary.

Together, however, we shall be on that day,
And see one another in joyous array,
Aunt Sue will be happy sent to heaven to dwell,
Will she be upset to see son Bill sent to hell?

No, resurrected, we will fully see
God's justice and his plan be manifest;
Our hearts will have such knowledge so that we will be
Aware God's workings of all things are best.

Feed Us Forever

In midst of transience
You do not change;
You speak and have spoken,
Your sheep have their range.

You call us to follow
The love You have shown;
Though strayed from Your pathway,
We are never alone.

You taught us the love
There's no health in us without;
That in coming to You
We will not be cast out.

You fed the five thousand,
Told us what we must do,
And offered the Living Bread
Of life ever with You.

Still give us Your sustenance
As we worship together;
Give Your food and Your drink, Lord,
That will feed us forever.

On *Colossians* 3:3

MY days increase in knowledge of His love;
LIFE seems more rare, enriched, as days decrease;
IS there a message coming from above
HIDDEN in heart awaiting its release?
IN my Lord's suffering, death, and rise
CHRIST gave the pattern that He bade us heed:
WITH sacrifice He teaches where love lies.
GOD, as belief grows, meets our inmost need.
PRAISE Him from Whom all blessings flow,
HIM we grow closer to as our days go.

MEETING ON THE ROAD

Who is that with you on this road of life
where change is inborn, irresistible?
The field's wheat is not ready to be gleaned;
you pass by with little notice as you walk,
sorrowed by news of suffering and loss.
You've lost the one your hopes were pinned upon,
but rumors say He could be yet alive.

Who is that stranger who has joined you now,
wanting to listen to your puzzled minds?
He tells you sacred things of prophets past,
that Jesus himself would suffer and die,
then would be raised again into His glory.

O wondrous! How He's set your hearts on fire
just when you've had and lost such gifts of love.
O moment pure! That stranger moves to go,
but at your urging stops to pass the night.

O night of doubt when hope has crept in heart;
at table when He blessed and broke the bread,
your eyes were opened to their greatest sight.

O travelers heart-weary in life's quest,
who is that with you that can give you rest?

TREES, REVISITED

How odd a twist of things there came to be
That man first fell by eating of the tree—
Knowledge of good and evil had he then,
And with it came awareness of his sin.

Another tree within the garden lay—
The tree of life was also out of play;
It offered life forever if he ate
This food forbidden in his fallen state.

God to prevent this prospect cast him out,
And man had wandered earth in quite a drought.
It is a mystery beyond our ken,
To know the many ways of God toward men:

To end His punishment God sent His Son,
Who on a tree for us eternity has won.

Your Will Be Done

Your will be done, Lord,
here in my everydayness.
Help me to know the fullness of
Your resurrection's meaning
within my heart and being.
Protect me from the evil
that is Your absence;
bring me to know
the presence of your everlasting joy.

*Thou hast made us for
Thyself, O Lord, and our
heart is restless until it
finds rest in Thee.*

—St. Augustine—

REST IN THY LOVE

Thou hast made us, and not just for ourselves;
Through Thy divine intent we find us here;
And when into Thy purposes we delve,
We rely upon Thy Word's presence ever near.

With restless hearts we struggle day by day
To know Thy will for what our lives should be.
We pray Thee, Lord, to take our sins away,
And draw our hearts toward Thee into eternity.

Then when called heavenward unto Thy breast,
We will have found indeed, O Lord, our hearts' true rest.

Quest for Unity

"…that they may be one,
even as we are one," said our Lord there,
often repeating the word "one"
in His high priestly prayer.

What once had been a unity of thought
among believers of the Word
is now insufficiently sought
and still is broken, blurred.

A God-sent mission showed
the Father's love and plan;
but sin and lack of unity,
are yet the work of man.

May we all listen closely to Thy prayer, O Lord,
to lessons given us at Thy Last Supper's board.
May Thou in our lives and churches that oneness yet instill,
that we may find Thy unity and love within Thy will.

PLEASING THE LORD

"May it please the Lord," the bishop once said;
His wish has resonated in my mind:
There should be more occasions we could find
to which it could apply to actions yet ahead.

I've done more than a few things not thereby approved,
and through repentance had those sins removed.

But there is in this world much war and strife,
and sins, cruel acts, and misdemeanors all are rife.

Yet there is so much good, also, to recommend
that doing good would please the Lord and us befriend,

May we show such kindness and love in one accord
that all our thoughts and words and deeds may please the Lord.

THE JOURNEY

Friend, go with me through
the muck of this material world;
We'll cross our sufferings,
as we would cross a bridge
between our present and more noble things.

We'll feel our feet more firmly drawn
toward the white, beckoning sands
of heaven's shore; we'll cast away
all disappointments as we journey forth
beyond limits of logic and our fears
into the Spirit's everlasting life.

As we embrace the drawing of God's love for us,
we'll see the meaning of our lives has been
to journey toward the goal of God,
toward our abode with Him.

Genuine contemplation comes as
a spontaneous, unexpected moment,
a sudden springing toward God that
shoots like a spark from a burning coal.

—from *The Cloud of Unknowing,*
modernized and edited by Bernard Bangley—

REFINING LOVE

Our souls at best are sparks toward God,
the ashes cling behind;
the residue is left in sod;
the spark will be refined.

In moments as we focus on His love
we grow less earthly and more free of dross;
drawn by the winds of Spirit to our home above,
enabled by His sacrifice on Cross.

We'll know His love by being warmed
by His refining fires;
as we come near His joy we 'll be transformed,
and hear eternal music that His love inspires.

Released from prison of our cold, dark clay,
we will adore the presence of His love's pure ray.

UPLIFTED

It was a precipice of thought—
I pondered on the state of man;
What centuries of strife had wrought
Upon each country, tribe, or clan.

Should we with energy and zest persist to strive
Through pain and suffering to find a lasting love,
And keep our dreams and hopes of earth alive,
Or should we set our hearts on heaven's joys above?

Problems and pleasures here give meaning to our life.
But only by contrast to better or worse things.
While I considered aspects of this world of strife,
A breath of sudden joy gave my heart wings.

Instead of attention downward toward earth's base,
I felt my thoughts and aims drawn upward by His grace.

The Presence

We stand upon the sands of life, open to You
O God whose endless love You have for us in store;
You did death's boundary and sin undo;
the waves of heaven break on our hearts' shore,
the rustling of Your Spirit stirs our souls' core.

You've shown us how even a suffering can bring
its opposite even to this world below;
may we unto thy glory ever grateful praises sing
for all the gifts that You on us bestow
when we within our hearts Your Presence know.

Promises of Faith

Sometimes we doubt the promise of our faith;
From brute to beautiful our life can be;
We know full well death's dark reality,
But we forget the words our Master saith.

What if the world was made this way
To lead to further faith in Him?
We see through glasses dark and dim,
Reach out from memories of mire and clay.

Is there a darkness where He can't show light?
There is a future brightness fear obscures;
More search of soul may show that faith endures,
And honest doubt can lead us out of night.

Believe what doubting Thomas God commands:
"Put out your fingers here and see my hands."

EDIFICE OF SOUL

Meaning itself is key to our being's quest;
whether we choose our purposes in life
or they're presented to us, we understand
they're made of values known, deeds done,
beauties felt, or sufferings, transmuted into will
in forms we can retrieve, remember, relive,
or see relived in actions like
taking the right path at the propitious time,
or sharing the beauty of the sunset's glow,
or in shaking the hand of one who's helped us
or whom we've helped, or seeing someone
sacrifice himself for others, or discovering
the truth that life is hard, that love and life
can be as fleeting in their passing as
a comet with its trail of dust that flashes by.
Yet we build up, within, an edifice of soul
through which we begin to see possibilities
that lead us to belief and to understanding
that here on earth we may know only a little part
of the truth, beauty, power, and love intended
for us, that we can here endure only so much
suffering, that what we most need to see is
that love was given, suffering was done for us once
so that we could know that our ultimate meaning
comes from the sacrifice of One Who understood
the limitations of our ways and surmounted them,
offering His love and then surrounding us
with everlasting arms.

Lord, let us rest this day in love and peace;
Keep us from all wrong and controversies;
Let our hearts be ever thankful for Thy love,
And give us that due sense of all Thy mercies.

POEMS OF LOVE AND LOSS

LOVE'S HEIGHTS

Long searched I for the flowers of delight
In mountain meadows with their bright bouquet,
To give you just a token of the way
My heart feels joyful when I hold you tight.

The flowers green and golden, blue and white,
That first are beauties of our happy day,
Become examples of our life's decay,
Though I present them in a lover's rite.

It is more constant love that stays the night;
Trust and commitment must we let hold sway;
Devotion shared will then our fears allay,
And, steadfast, set our love and lives aright.

Blend that which most engenders love that's whole,
Not only sight and sense, but mind and soul.

Love's Reach

A look into your eyes so welcomes me,
The clasp of hand that wants no more to go,
The smile that lifts my heart to let me see
A oneness possible to live, and love, and grow.

It is with guidance of Almighty's hand
That we reach out with love as if to say
We can now know its meaning, understand,
Like coming home after long years away.

Within God's open arms we sheltered are;
There is about us love's infinity,
Because He reached into our lives so far
That we are brought to His eternity.

It is more love than human hearts can bear
To see Him guide us here on earth, then lead us there.

HOMECOMING

I want to go again into the bright October,
into the hills once home,
to find out something more of who I am
now that I've lost you.

It's not enough to love life in the leaf's
green spring and red and yellow fall;
we need someone to share the road's turns,
shared memories,
and the crisp moment of the now.

I am a slate wiped clean of almost all
but grief and fragments you'd restored,
yet I will go to greet
faces and names I haven't seen and heard
in forty-five years' time.

And they will say, "You lost your wife, I heard,"
"So sorry," and "What are you doing now?"
but not "Who are you now?" or "Who
are you becoming?"

I'd like to think I could go home again,
passing the red clay and the mountain streams,
a stone, a leaf, a door… a life…
But who will I be, without you here beside me,
you purpose of all voyaging and being home?

SAYING GOODBYE

I loved you in all seasons, out of time;
You came like breath of spring and brought such joy
That I was like a fighter in his prime
Whom nothing but your loss could now destroy.

Across togetherness of years, your smile
Knitted the fragments that my life had been;
Your growing grace and beauty, all the while,
Let sun of summer into life again.

But with another growth the autumn came,
Making the fragrance of the rose more rare;
In face of pending loss, we loved the same,
And even sorrow, shared, seemed sweet to bear.

It's now the hardest thing my heart can try:
To hold your love within and say goodbye.

Love is the ultimate
and highest goal.
—Victor Frankl—

THREE LOVES

Physical love brings pleasures that will fade
yet stay in moment and in memory's green springs,
and like great music can our souls invade,
or move us softly as the music clings.

Friendship and love for others bless our day;
loving them as ourselves is our command.
When we argue and lose a friend along the way,
we thus erode ourselves like ocean shore's lost sand.

Love of the spirit, love's abiding flame,
is sown with seed of longing in our heart.
With sacrifice of self, love's power we proclaim
and find a love that cannot then depart.

Love is the ultimate and highest goal,
where spirit builds a kingdom in our soul.

My Music

My heart was captured by a song
That never stopped all day—
I felt my soul to it belong;
Its music's majesty held sway.

The river's murmured joy I caught;
The pealing bells of church—
The haunting sounds of flute I sought;
Strong guitar rhythms graced my music's search.

I heard the symphony of ocean's shore,
Lone sound of loon upon the lake,
The jazz of juke box and the dancer's floor:
These thus within me did sweet music make.

In all these sounds and more I did rejoice,
But I loved most the music of your voice.

Many Universes

We were always together, though apart
in time and place. I, though yet unborn,
felt myself there with you; I came alive
at your first smile, cried with you at
your unfulfilled desires, played in your shadows,
slept with you in your depth of innocence and sleep.

Our meeting was
a shift of time and place,
a movement of the universe for us by which
God gave us to each other, as He gives
and will give. Oh, how He helps us shape
our own existence, showing us
patterns of recurrence and rebirth.

True, there are many universes, some in which
I never met you by the ocean's shore, nor held
you close along a starlit, windswept mountain path;
universes in which I lost you and could not
recover my delight and inspiration from your eyes
as I do now.

May the future shape us further, bringing fruit of joy
ripe with the perfection of all time,
and oh, my love, may I assure you this:
Even in the universes where I did not write this poem,
I loved you and will love you without words.

Where Ashes Lie

I write this where your ashes lie, and know
That you are one with the Eternal here
In this church garden.

Yours is St. Francis's peace, the peace of all
That see God's face. I wonder if
You ever in some sense look back below
There from the wholeness you now have
To here where injury, doubt, despair,
Darkness, and sadness often dim our paths.

Reading his prayer, I think of how you are
Already an instrument of God's peace,
And here in this small garden I am humbled
To know how much I have received from Him and you,
And how little I have given.

"For it is in giving that one receives,"
Says the prayer, and you gave so much love
That you now have heaven as your soul's reward,
And I, having known your depth of love,
Can find a joy in knowledge of your depth of peace.

Love's Statement

Life is a statement being made by Love;
Love says, "I'd like to know your very soul;"
And Life responds, "I'm here because of you."

These two build up our personality,
Make us unique and real in who we are.
We're not defined by death or by our selves,
But by Love's giving meaning to our lives.

In midst of change, give Love priority,
And you will achieve the best Life you can be.

Sometimes we feel a breeze of nothingness
Approach the moments of our earthly stay,
But Love says, "I'll prove superior";
Life boasts, "I know my worth."

WRIGHTSVILLE BEACH

Here where we met,
here at the sea's bright symphony,
the water's highlights and its shadows stretch
to a seeming infinity.

Waiting for the sun to burn
illimitably into me, renew,
I can't turn back again this tide of time;
instead, I elevate my eyes and memories of you,
my ocean's treasure.

You're in the joy I seek,
which like the pure, white, silent sail I see
fades in the distance from my limited, lost shore,
while up above, your soul, to show the path of love,
soars with the wings it always wanted and dreamed of.

Inspired by Sun and Ocean

Our mood is elevated by the rising tide,
here as we walk upon the ocean's shore,
alternating dips in sea with strides in sand.
With brown pelicans gliding slowly in a vee,
we clasp hands and say,
"I love you" and "I love you more," as if
it were a game, but meaning every word.
The sun is warm upon us now,
and we are ripened by it and the glow of afternoon.
I'll spend the evening's effervescence in your arms,
sensing the rhythm and the warmth like that of
the ocean's caressing and withdrawing waves.
We are so inspired by sunset's radiant setting
and ocean's recurrent movements and massage,
that we wish never to cease this day, this love.

PATHWAYS OF LOVE

These were some pathways of our love:
the ocean brought us together as we felt
its soft undulations, and with the waves'
endless returning we too came back frequently
into that summer sea in which our love began.

Soon there were mountain pathways we traveled
just off the Blue Ridge Parkway, where, in morning mists,
the rhododendrons thrived, opening their beauty
as we drew closer in our life together.

Longer paths took us often abroad, where Europe's
cities and countrysides revealed their treasures,
whether at Edinburg's Tattoo, Rome's Forum, or
enjoying a canal barge trip in Burgundy,
or strolling down Montmartre or the Champs-Élysée,
you and I explored these highways of our joy.

The path of pain began when cancer struck;
we traced its progress in a muter tone,
pressing these later grapes of our life's wine
into a different and subdued mode of hope
shown forth in preciousness of love near loss
in quiet times of singing and of praising God.

When Love calls, one roadway leads to a different
reality, and after sharing your love with me
these many avenues and years of life,
the Lord called and you took His pathway home.

Your Love in Spring

When April cast its promises of green
about the earth in its awakening,
I picked for you wildflowers I could glean;
I had the beauty of your love in spring.

I sang to you all songs that I could sing;
my heart wanted to give you everything.
You said "yes" when I offered you my ring;
I had the beauty of your love in spring.

My heart was like a kite upon your string;
you were the highest joy that love could bring.
It is to your memory I now cling;
I had the beauty of your love in spring.

WEIGHT OF ABSENCE

Their branches overladen with the rain,
these gardenias and magnolias miss
your guiding presence, miss your smile and sigh,
while you inhaled their fragrance.
Your world was ever green and white,
just as our world together uttered joy;
then for the longest you held on
until you knew the everyness of things,
and I am left
to watch the weighted flowers bend unpicked.

A Villanelle of Love

I love you, dear, and want to show my love each day,
The beauty, joy, and happiness that our love brings,
Life's treasures that I have with you today.

I love you, dear, much more than I can say;
I hear the music of your voice and my heart sings;
I love you, dear, and want to show my love each day.

My debt of love to you I can with love repay:
I have love's riches beyond that of kings,
Life's treasures that I have with you today.

Each day with you is like a day in May;
Your kisses and your touch give my heart wings;
I love you, dear, and want to show my love each day.

Without your love my hopes in life are gray,
But with your love I have delight in all good things,
Life's treasures that I have with you today.

When we're on the dance floor and our close bodies sway,
My life is like a kite on your love's strings.
I love you dear, and want to show my love each day,
Life's treasures that I have with you today.

LIGHT RAIN

There is light rain tonight as I bemoan your loss.
I loved you ever in the rain; now you are one
with elemental things, and I am left
in prison of myself, remembering how
the two of us had shuddered in rain's joy.
You're in the joy now, and not just that of rain;
I must take heart that both our happiness
and suffering here had and still have
meaning, were and yet remain
a part of God's plan that will not be lost
but lived and died into, as we were shown the way
by Him who saved us for eternal life.

TO AN AUNT

You were the aunt who, when I was very young,
took me on walks enjoying local woods,
paths, and hillsides full of mountain flowers.
You went through difficulties in later life,
transferred to Manhattan's busy stores,
where you saved all the books that you could find
to ship them back home to your mountain place,
which would be a bookstore on your return.

From your bookstore beside the waterwheel
you came to help our family in its time of need.
My life was troubled; perhaps I could have tried
harder to help you find a safer home
more suitable to your condition and your age.

We always wondered whether you had jumped
toward the car that hit you, which then ran away,
or if the car had gone out of its proper lane.
Your painful final dozen years found little peace,
but I was there to help you through them as I could.

I inherited your books after you died,
and came across a message for the future me
you'd added to the margins of a special book;
You said, "One day you'll read this when you're old,
and know the feelings that I'm feeling now."

Forgive me, if the dead can yet forgive;
My heart knows you're in a better place.
Know that I love you; may you in heaven see
how much your memory and life have meant to me.

Mountainside Orchard

The trees are still there on the mountainside,
and in the fall one fewer
person to pick their apples.
And can I ever go again unto those hills
seeking the apples' and the air's crisp joy
without you, oh my love?
Perhaps in heaven there are places where
we'll share the fullness this life only hinted at,
and yet relive the moments of insights of love
here in these earthly places where they somehow matter so,
and you will be beside me on the mountainside.

HAIKU
AND OTHER POEMS

The coldest day of winter—
some blossoms have opened
on the breath of spring bush.

Sunset in winter:
cattails in the pond become
prisoners of ice.

In the quiet rain
my love for you is nourished
like the earth in spring.

Together in March wind:
my heart soars heavenward—
a kite on your string.

Ancient live oak—
How have your branches weathered
so many storms of life?

May coolness in rain:
I shiver in the closeness
of your embrace.

Forget the mosquitoes:
Let's not hurry in—
I see some fireflies!

The scent of jasmine—
how bittersweet
this first spring without you.

In the dark of night
my being is enlightened by
the candle of Your presence.

We kneel together—
Your presence in bread and wine
fills our hearts with love.

A masked bandit
climbs up our deck rail—
a raccoon at the feeder!

The dog and the bear
fail to maintain their shapes—
the cloud's form changes!

This rainy morning there
under the weeping willow—
two lovers kissing.

The marsh in summer—
life somehow abounds
despite pollution.

The beast in the park
opens waiting arms and jaws—
a praying mantis!

Those horrible sounds
coming from the gutter's base
a bullfrog tonight!

That pine cone has grown
much smaller since yesterday—
the squirrel's belly's full!

August yellow swirl
alights on the pond's surface:
leaf or butterfly?

October pathway:
this second year without you;
Memories are scattered leaves.

As I've grown older
I'd rather not have them now:
these icy days of winter.

Vivid seashore find:
this pearly conch shell—
put it to your ear and listen!

The advancing knight
has been lost to the castle—
the chess game proceeds.

All at once on the branch
comes blue, red, and yellow-green—
a painted bunting!

Late graveyard visit:
Tombstones gleam more brightly
In autumn's full moon.

Monastery's halls:
the voice of God is speaking
within the silence.

IMAGES RELEASED

Images have meaning, speak aloud;
each, with its own voice, has a life within.
I've stored them through the years;
now, as I grow older, ripened, I release them
as I would a bird from cage, ready to fly
into the light with fresh reality and scope
at my command:
a windswept meadow,
Venice with bright skies,
a lakeshore in the rain,
your eyes,
a mountain stream—
they come before the canvas of my art
with newfound meaning as they're summoned.
One image bears its music; one a sight;
and others—fragrance, feeling, memory—
the rainbow-colored gleam as sea meets land,
sunlight encountered quickly on a winding road,
your smile,
blue bearded irises in May.
To work their vivid power, I refine their gold
and launch them forth on laden ships of poetry.

An Island in Time

Here where the island meets Atlantic's roar
and pelicans glide with grace above the waterway,
I have been waiting for seawater touching shore
that brings a kiss of foam with its short stay.
I feel a transitoriness of time
as ebbing water takes the foam away.

I am cleansed slowly of my loneliness
as if baptized by these foam bubbles in my hand
that bathe my life with ocean's light caress
and leave all weight of worries in the sand.
Am I that foam that sits upon reality
with meaning founded upon nothingness?

I find my meaning in the love I share
and in faith's journey that keeps hope alive;
Oceans of living water are everywhere
life's possibilities, a shore on which we strive.
Our brevity is bulwarked by wise choice of acts,
and we are made ourselves the moment that we dare.

LOOKING BACK

There is a warmth in looking back
over these centuries of kin as I encounter
this faded photograph of you, an old woman
folding a full century in your crossed arms,
cane in hand, seated, black hat upon your head.
To think how your lifespan reached back almost
to that of my fifth great-grandfather who fought
in the Revolution—that you, his granddaughter,
survived almost to the time of my own birth!
The stories you could tell, your memories—
Your face is wizened yet is wise; it's filled
with wonderment and quiet fortitude
by having seen much beauty, love, and suffering,
from seeing all the change
your century and more has brought you.
What would you think of me if things
were the other way around, with you viewing me?
What would you think to learn
that I was your first cousin
five times removed, searching our history?
We'd talk of our connections, lost ones of our kin,
and marvel at what time and God had wrought.
I wish I'd known you then—
as you may know me now.

THE ART OF POETRY

Poets turn words to wonders on display
In gathered sheaves of poetry;
Their scythe cuts stubble carefully away,
And yields in garnered grain their poem's majesty.

With chosen word each in its proper place,
See symbol, meaning, metaphor abound;
Right tone when added gives the poem grace,
And rhythm, rhyme luxuriate the sound.

Read, listen closely to the poem's art—
It will speak truly to your mind and heart.

GARDENS IN WINTER

I enter this bare garden of winter
by a gate with failing post
and weakened hinges, like my own tired legs.
Even the weeds have died, leaving dry husks.

And as I think on whether to prepare
to plant again next year,
I think of other gardens, other times.
with varied range of purpose and event.

When world was innocence and spring,
Was it you, Earth, uttering such green as I came forth
to feel first love within your readied grounds?
How I embraced the sunshine of her arms
and like a bellarmine bore on my breast
the bright medallion of her love!

From a later garden, how I was joyed to eat
from summer's bounty at the sensual feast, a riot
of melon, cucumber, and grape—came further
into a paradise of knowing, not of innocence.

Beyond the fig's ripeness, should we stay or go?
How could we in a different world
find means to be and yet to grow,
toward a perfection without Earth's decay?
It may be that the best of being's not to feel
beyond this fullness—here our lives and words
die in time's grasp like garden crops, leaving only
a blaze of color like the autumn leaf.

Wind-scattered leaves, what does it mean for us to be
so fleetingly in love with time, yet longing for
its ending, as in music? We're fixed in time,
yet always needing time to bring us to
whatever eternity awaits.

Earth, you can't deliver us, no, nor transform,
however much we'll miss your summer rains
that give a shiver to our being's sap.
It is a wholeness that we seek
beyond the movement of the years and time.

Yet I am strangely beckoned by this earthly stay;
perhaps the purpose of this place and time's to show
that here alone can love be manifest
in sharpest contrasts: life and death,
matter and spirit, time
and eternity; that the best ground is here
for opposites to meet and new things grow.

Was there an intersect, where Absolute
came to us in our time, to draw us to itself,
that worked its way through dark Gethsemane?
Gardens make us think, some say, of how
the world was lost to us, but Gethsemane had seen
a depth of suffering from which
ultimate love and life for others could spring forth.

At my small garden's edge, bidding my heart lie fallow
for more fruit, I find with thankfulness and awe
acceptance of this unbounded love. Sometimes I feel
closest to heaven when in gardens' grounds.
Their stories bright and dark of earth and love are ones
we must submit to and then plant again,
both outward and within, for head and heart and hand
have much to do with most already done.

It Really Doesn't Matter

It really doesn't matter
In the night and in the rain
That arms that held are missing
And memories are in vain.
That faith once held is shattered
And love comes not again,
But it really doesn't matter
In the night and in the rain.

It really doesn't matter
In the night and in the rain
When against the blast of living
No poetry can sustain;
When the moment's proud possession
Offers nothing to retain,
It really doesn't matter
In the night and in the rain.

The Coldest Day

"Today's the coldest it's ever been," the sheriff said,
"and I've got fourteen people here that's dead.
The roads are all closed now for miles around,
and there's a foot of snow cov'ring the ground.

The bus driver had failed to see ice at the curve;
the truck driver had seen the bus too late to swerve.
It careened over the rail, an eighty-yard dive;
so far we've found five passengers alive."

The deputy shook his head and then replied,
"How can we tell these parents that their children died?"
With sounds of sirens piercing the cold air,
the scene's mood turned from hope into despair.

They'd helped one girl who'd managed to survive intact.
she'd had good fortune that most others lacked.
But most had bodies broken to such sad degree
that blood mingled with snow in their white agony.

The sheriff and deputy now had turned to go;
somehow the screams they'd heard seemed strange through
snow.
The bitter cold they'd fought so long against
had hit them hard and lowered their defense.

Snow and ice had worsened chance of further rescue.
The sheriff said, "I have a real hard duty yet to do.
This is the worst and coldest day it's ever been,
and now I have to notify the next of kin."

The Moment

Take a moment of your life and freeze the frame;
Look for the quality of tone you thought was there—
That you kept reaching for but seldom held—
Hiding behind existence.

When the light seems right,
When streaks of sunlight penetrate the dark
And kindle hope and memory,
Insight and action are one.

You can preserve the image for a while
Against the vagaries of change and loss;
Press hard the shutter of this moment now,
Until only the beauty remains.

THE LARGER PATTERN

The past is rich with possibility;
Who is that person hiding up your family tree?
Perhaps a knowledge of your past will set you free,
Reveal a broader part of you in genealogy.

So try your hand at it and do a search;
You may be well rewarded for your good research.
The past is rich with possibility;
You might discover you relate to me!

HUMMINGBIRD, FAREWELL

I miss you, my humming friend;
You buzzed me often with your probing beak.
I'm sorry that our meetings had to end—
Your feeder can't stay up another week.

The landlord's said no feeders on the balcony,
No colored lights as well;
It seems an excess of conformity
That's forced me at this time to say farewell.

You'll have to find a flower or a bug
To eat in place of nectar that's homemade.
I'd offer you some sweetness from my mug,
But I don't want your diet to degrade.

In all, it feels there must be something wrong
To have to silence any humming song.

The Feeding of Bluebirds

A striking blue with breast of reddish brown,
You came to our birdhouse to settle down,
And with your sweet beloved built a nest;
It was not long to be a place of rest.

The top of your new home received a cup
That would hold mealy worms my wife put in
Almost as fast as you would eat them up;
You two would soon a family begin.

It was hard work to feed your growing group;
You played protector when my wife came near,
As she approached the feeder you would swoop,
And then divebomb her in pretended fear.

It was joyous, reenacted comedy—
I'm glad she had to feed them and not me!

The Gentleness of Deer

I saw you standing in the dwindling forest patch;
you looked at me with eyes of tenderness,
not running from me on your cloven hooves.
But you might need to run from some who think it's sport
to kill you, or from those angered when you eat their plants.
You with your two fauns, spotted with brushstrokes of white,
will soon go quietly into your narrow woods,
while I think of the gentleness of you,
forced here in man's encroachment on your habitat.
You've shared with me a moment of your being's grace,
and I repay you only with my wonderment.

Memory Care

I have been watching all
the people going by;
they go up and down the hall,
but I just can't think why.

Sometimes I go with them, hoping to find
Something we're looking for,
Right now it doesn't come to mind.
We just keep walking but can't get past the door.

There are some moods that seem like fear
when on my bed I lie;
somehow it means so much to be here,
but I can't remember why.

The Hills of Home

When I was a boy it was my joy
To roam the hills and mountainside;
I did not need to have a toy,
Nor did I need to have a guide.

I simply needed to explore all paths and streams
And every cave and valley I could see.
Beauty of mountain flowers filled my dreams;
The mountains and the foothills were my place to be.

I even climbed a hill to get to school:
We were the "Hilltoppers" of R.S. Central High;
We learned to do things by the golden rule,
And "Go, Hilltoppers" was our strong war cry.

My thoughts are sweeter than the honeycomb
When I go on my way to roam the hills of home.

MEDITERRANEAN SCENE

Ah, painter, you have captured well the scene
of this sunlit Mediterranean garden yard.
Palms, villas, evergreens, and sails reach toward sky.
Bright colored flowers meet us on each side of walk,
split only by the pathway of increasing light
leading our eyes down to the gate near golden mean,
suggesting unseen steps to the blue sea,
whose waters reach to misty mountains opposite,
where homes at base will offer similar views
almost as beautiful as the one you've showcased here.

FULL TIDE

The full tide of the soul is felt at times;
Luminous moments hint at life's mystery
and etch themselves into our memories:

Les Baux at full moon on the mountaintop,
Mont St. Michel when tide encompasses,
a London walk that suddenly comes upon
portions of buildings left from Roman days,
a foggy glow of early daylight at Cades Cove,
deep thought in an old churchyard by a grave,
a walk inside a glacier near Mont Blanc,
a Christmas service in a stable near Versailles.

These and like moments edify, build up our lives;
They help us know the wonders of our world,
give solace and delight, help give us strength against
the winds of change that in the end take all away.

Time of Conflict

With present time of conflict, anxiety, and strife,
affecting affairs of state and personal life,
with so much rage and hate at work, we seem to be
a country of confrontational polarity.

A lack of morals is the surest sign
that our country's standard is now in decline;
When people rejoice or run riot at someone's demise
a portion of our nation's fabric dies.

Though we have heritage of hate as well as love,
there is a line of conduct we must rise above.
To be a land both civilized and free,
we must prepare to withstand anarchy.

We must, in midst of struggles that increase,
strive to turn hatred and confusion into peace.
Peace is the holy grail we seek to find,
with changes of the heart as well as mind.

With proper education, love, and empathy,
we may yet turn disorder toward unity.

Lines Written at Wilmington National Cemetery

Here where white tombs arise from green of earth,
We feel the pride and honor due those buried here.
They fought or gave with all their beings' worth
For family, friends, and country that were dear.

These dead are gone now to a brighter home;
They feel the weight and sorrow of the earth no more.
They are not captives of the coffins' loam;
They've reached eternal light of heaven's shore.

Their honor and their accolades remain,
Reminding us that freedom is not free,
That these brave heroes did not die in vain;
They live on now and always in our memory.

The Truths of Things

The truths of things we were not yet to see
appear before us as our lives unfold;
we see now by the aid of memory.

It's happened throughout our history:
In youth we lacked skills and could not behold
The truths of things we were not yet to see.

We struggle to know things we can't foresee,
but in the school of life we are enrolled;
we see now by the aid of memory.

They say the truths of things will set you free,
but life has its conditions that withhold
the truths of things we were not yet to see.

In life's choices there is no guarantee,
yet our wisdom and our faith have made us bold;
we see now by the aid of memory.

The joys that we remember are the key
to happiness in life as we grow old;
The truths of things we were not yet to see
we see now by the aid of memory.

Open Up

Let your heart be light, my creative friend,
Sing through all moments of discouragement.
Open all windows of the heart and mind

　　　　　　　　impounding you.

Break open all barriers to imagination's force

　　　　　　　　confounding you.

Open yourself to colors of the spectrum's joy

　　　　　　　　surrounding you.

Hear all the joyful instruments of earth's chorus

　　　　　　　　resounding in you.

Refresh the morning with your shouted song

　　　　　　　　abounding in you.

Achieve the art your life is giving you

　　　　　　　　astounding you.

EXPLORATIONS

One path has scattered golden yellow leaves,
fallen in profusion from bending trees. Another
season's road shows margins of an early spring,
camellias so delicate in their pink and white
that they amaze and hold us in their beauty's grasp.
Whatever season's pathway that we take,
enrichment is the sum and goal of all our ways.
We should continue to explore
the mystery in each flower and leaf
of our existence, as if more beauty
could be revealed than we can see.
These memories are explorations
of where our hearts have led us;
our imagination blooms
and merges with our memories, so to feed
our present with a cool, rich freshness
like a renewal of the leaves in spring.
We are a composite of all
the dreams of earth; we find
the beauty of our work and loves,
even in the sufferings we've transmuted
into strengths; we will in looking back
to these blossoms of our accumulated selves
see what the meanings of our lives and memories
have been and are, as we
continue to explore our possibilities.

TRANSLATIONS

THE STEPS

Your footsteps, children of my silence,
So saintly, slowly made
Toward the bed of my vigilance,
Come quietly and icily conveyed.

Being of purity, shadow divine,
How sweet are these your footsteps you withhold!
God! How all gifts I guessed to be so fine
Come to me on these naked feet and cold!

If from your offered lips you do prepare
For my mind's inmost resident this bliss
To calm him with your tender care,
You nourish him more fully with a kiss,

Rush not this tender action new
so sweet to be and not to be—
For I have lived to wait for you;
Your steps were but the heart of me.

Translated version of the French poem
"Les Pas," by Paul Valéry

PETIT AIR
II

As my hope springs to that place
indomitably, wildly is bound
to burst out above in lost space
with fury and no sound

a voice strange to the wood,
followed by no echo,
the bird one never could
again in this life know.

This musician of unrest,
this one who dies in doubt,
if not from his, my breast
the worst sob has gushed out,

Will he remain, though torn,
on some path yet unworn?

---

*Translated from the French poem of the
same title by Stéphane Mallarmé*

To Christ Crucified

I am not moved, my God, so much to win
The heaven that you promised me,
Nor is it by the hell which I so fear to see
That I am moved to cease my sin.

You move me, Lord, move me to think of when
They nailed you to your cross; you had to be
So wounded and despised to such degree;
Your suffering and your death—**You** move me then.

And, most of all, **Your love**—it moves me so
that even if no heaven is, nor hell below,
I'd fear you still; my love would ever flow.

You need not give me more, my love to grow:
and even if I lacked that hope I hope for, know
I'd love you still; my love would never go.

---

*This anonymous 16th Century Spanish sonnet is
adapted from the prose translation by J.M. Cohen in*
The Pilgrim Book of Spanish Verse, Revised Edition,
(1965)*, and is here put into its original rhyme pattern.*

THE VIRGIN, QUICK, AND BEAUTIFUL TODAY

The virgin, quick, and beautiful today
Will it tear for us—wing-drunken blow—
This hard, forgotten lake haunted by frost below
With the clear ice of flights not gotten underway?

A swan of former times remembers that it's he
Who though magnificent lacks hope of being free
When sterile winter illumined ennui
With his not having sung the land in which to be.

All his neck will shake off this white agony
Inflicted by space on the bird who'd deny
But not the horror of clay his plumage is caught by.

Phantom whose brilliance assigns him to this bourn,
The swan, arrayed in useless exile, stills himself
In the cold dream which has been filled with scorn.

Translated from the sonnet by Stéphane Mallarmé,
"Le vierge, le vivace, et le bel aujourd'hui"

THE SCENERY

I had dreamed of loving; I still love, but love
no longer is a bouquet of lilac and rose
loading with perfume the forest that shows
a flame without turns burning in the path above.

I had dreamed of loving; I love, but love that's there
is no longer tempest where lightning imports
its pyres over the castles, confuses and distorts,
and fleeing, lights its farewell in the public square.

It is the flint of fire under my steps at night,
the word no dictionary can translate aright,
this cloud in sky, the drossy foam of sea.

In ageing, all becomes rigid and brightly lit,
boulevards without names, cords without knit;
I feel myself become stiff with the scenery.

Translated from the French poem,
"Le Paysage," by Robert Desnos

I AM RIPE

The sun has warmed me for so many years
that I think my inmost being now is ripe,
and you will descend, Lord, to pluck me up
with your immense and naked hands.

I am mature and golden for your dream,
and I will navigate it like a moon
that travels through it shining brilliantly,
a star that's like a fruit in your pure night.

A cloud will then by chance blot out
my light for living, and in the rain
your sweet nectar, my being's very sap,
will fall to you, my Lord, like music's fall.

Then I will be dead, delivered
another time into the tomb of earth.
But, immortal blood, my living heart of red,
will burn anew within your future light.

---

*Translated from the Spanish poem
"Estoy Maduro," by José Luis Hidalgo*

SONNETS TO ORPHEUS, I, 19

Although the world quickly changes itself
like cloud formations,
all completed things fall
homeward to primeval ground.

Above change and process,
wider and freer,
your early song persists,
god with the lyre.

Sufferings have not been understood,
nor has love been learned,
and what in death goes from us

is not revealed.
Only the melodious song heard over land
hallows and celebrates.

Translated from the German of
Rainer Maria Rilke's "Die Sonette an Orpheus"
("Sonnets to Orpheus"), I, 19

SONNETS TO ORPHEUS, II, 29

Silent friend who has come so far,
feel how your breath increases all of space.
In the beams of the dark bell loft
let your voice grow louder. That which resounds in you

grows stronger from this nourishment. Go through
your transformation like this bell's movement, in and out.
What is your most sorrowful loss experienced?
If your drink is bitter, turn yourself to wine.

Be power in this night of vast darkness,
magical power at this crossroads
of your life and senses.

And if the earth forgets you,
say to it quietly: I flow.
To the brisk water say: I am.

---

*Translated from the German of
Rainer Maria Rilke's "Die Sonette an Orpheus"
("Sonnets to Orpheus"), II, 29*

El Desdichado

I am the obscure, the inconsolable, the widower,
The Prince of Aquitaine in the ruined tower:
My only star is dead;
My lute, star-studded,
Bears the black sun of melancholy's power.

In my night of the tomb,
You who've eased my heart's gloom,
Give me back the Pausilippe and Italian sea,
The flower that when I was forlorn so pleased me,
The trellis joining its vine with the rose in bloom.

Am I Love or Apollo?...Lusignan or Biron?
My forehead is still red with the kiss of the queen;
I have dreamed in the grotto where swims the siren.

I have twice crossed Acheron in victory,
On Orpheus' lyre warbling songs that are airy,
The sighs of the saints and the cries of the fairy.

From the French poem of the same title
by Gérard de Nerval

SUMMER

In the evening the cuckoo's lament
grows silent in the forest.
The grain inclines its head deeper,
The red poppy.

Darkening thunder threatens
over the hill.
The old cricket's song
dies away in the field.

The chestnut tree's leaves
no longer stir.
On the winding stair is heard
the rustle of your dress.

Silently the candle gleams
in the dim room;
a silver hand
puts out the light.

Starless, windless night.

From the German poem "Sommer"
("Summer") by Georg Trakl

SONG OF AUTUMN

With sobs long,
the violin's song
of autumn
wounds my heart
with a weary
monotone.

All suffocating and pale,
when the clock
sounds its tale,
I remember the days gone by,
and I cry.

And I let myself go
where the foul winds blow
carrying me in my grief
first here, then there
like the dead autumn leaf.

From the French "Chanson d'Automne"
by Paul Verlaine

A Prayer attributed to Brother Roger of Taizé

To look for you, Lord Christ, is to discover
that you have already been our lover
although we did not know it,
and by your Holy Writ
you gave us a good glimpse into
the way that we may better know and love you.

We know also how your love has pursued
and even met us in our inmost solitude.

Happy are they who lose themselves in you;
happy are they who come closer to you.

They place their trust in you as their hearts' choice;
You are the serene joy that makes their hearts rejoice.

---

*Note: I have added rhyme to this French
prayer attributed to Brother Roger of Taizé.*

ABOUT THE AUTHOR

LADSON BRIGHT, better known as Lad, is a native of Spindale, N.C., and a retired Instructor of English at Cape Fear Community College in Wilmington, NC, where he and his wife Joanmarie live.

He is author of a booklet of poems and photographs, *Pathways and Gradations* (1983) and of numerous articles printed in *Saints Alive*, the newsletter of All Saints Anglican Parish, Wilmington, N.C., of which he is a member. He has a BA in English from N.C. State University and an MA in Comparative Literature from UNC-Chapel Hill. Cover and internal photos are his.

www.ingramcontent.com/pod-product-compliance
Lightning Source LLC
Chambersburg PA
CBHW051324120626
46547CB00015B/2389